Lived-In Style

Lived-In Style

THE ART OF CREATING A FEEL-GOOD HOME

KI NASSAUER

With photography by Edmund Barr

CICO BOOKS

LONDON NEW YORK

First published in the United Kingdom
in 2023 by
Ryland Peters & Small
20–21 Jockey's Fields
London WC1R 4BW
and
341 E 116th Street
New York, NY 10029
www.rylandpeters.com

Designer: Paul Tilby
Senior Commissioning Editor:
   Annabel Morgan
Art Director: Sally Powell
Creative Director: Leslie Harrington
Production Manager: Gordana Simakovic

British Library Cataloguing-in-Publication
Data. A catalogue record for this book is
available from the British Library.

ISBN : 978-1-80065-214-9

Printed and bound in China.

MIX
Paper from
responsible sources
FSC® C106563

Contents

Introduction

Opposite: Equal parts cozy and beautiful, homeowner Memo Faraj says this bright-by-day, moody-by-night den is his favorite room. He turned its non-working fireplace into a warming vignette.

Above left: "I love figuring out the story behind a piece of antique furniture or object," says former Texas dealer Angie Cavalier, whose travels to France reshaped her perspective on living with history.

Above right: A dedicated thrifter, Memo Faraj has learned to scour every inch of a store for unexpected treasures, like a $3 carved rocking horse from a toy section that launched a collection.

What is *Lived-In Style*? Perhaps better defined as a way of living rather than a specific look, for some it may bring to mind the comfy reading chair you cozy up in next to the window with a stack of books waiting nearby. It might get you thinking about those soft, faded jeans you pull on every weekend, or the collection of found treasures displayed on your mantel. It's laid-back, comfortable, no-fuss and uniquely you. Moreover, lived-in style isn't about perfection, but rather about finding joy in the imperfections that give our lives, and our homes, their unmistakable character. It's mismatched and worn, used and repurposed, kind and respectful to the earth and its resources. And it's what all the homes in this book have in common, whether in the city or country; modern, traditional or something in between; budget-conscious or not. Rather than purchasing an entire living room from a catalog or copying a neighbor's perfectly appointed parlor, each homeowner has gathered pieces they love from here, there and everywhere and, over time, woven them together to create energizing spaces that are truly their own. I hope you'll be inspired to do the same.

Ki Nassauer

Common Ground

Opposite left: The purchase of a small portrait at her first flea-market visit sparked a lifelong love of antiques in Melanie Bendavid. Decades later, it mingles (near the twig chair) with countless other finds.

Opposite right: An anniversary gift from her husband, this hand-painted antique cabinet pays tribute to Kirsten Tangeros' Norwegian heritage and the traditional art of rosemaling.

This page: Johanna Brannan Lowe inherited this George III dresser from her mother. She recalls that her birthday and Christmas presents were always hidden inside, nestled among sweaters and old perfume bottles.

Nods to the Past

In with the old! These days, shopping opportunities for vintage, antique and thrifted furniture and accessories have become more plentiful, whether you haunt a local secondhand shop, plan a road trip to a famous flea market or hit up the ever-growing array of online sources—or all of the above. Not only are the items often more wallet-friendly than those you find in a big-box store, but in exchange for a little work getting them

home, or performing a few potential fix-ups, you're rewarded with one-of-a-kind furnishings and accessories that impart instant character. As featured homeowner Molly Bechert Kipp observes, "A room will remain unfinished until you put an antique in it." And this is where you can truly make an impact on the earth too. "My favorite pieces have been around for over 100 years and are just getting started," notes former antiques dealer Angie Cavalier. "Most new furniture will be in a landfill in 40–50 years' time."

An Editor's Eye

Some people have a knack for putting this with that and making it look great, but creating interesting rooms that work is a skill anyone can acquire. Of course, there are helpful tricks designers use that you can borrow when pulling together favorite things. When arranging furniture, for instance, be sure that the largest piece is the furthest away when you walk in a room, and all of the feet should fit on an area rug, if you have one, including dining chairs that are pulled out from the table. Groupings look best in odd numbers, and vignettes benefit from mixed materials, like wood, metal and glass. The center of a mirror or artwork should be 60in/152cm from the ground; if you're doing a gallery wall, build out from there so that you have a grounded focal point. But perhaps more important than anything is this: Be willing to experiment. Move things around. Mix and match. "Look for contrast and sympathy of objects," advises stylist and homeowner Johanna Lowe. "The more you go, the more you know," adds creative consultant Kaitlyn Coffee, who recommends frequent trips to thrift and antiques stores to hone your eye.

Above left: As a maximalist who loves to fill his home with art of all kinds, Memo Faraj prevents his collections from overwhelming by holding out for prize specimens. And, when he finds one, it replaces a less-precious piece.

Left: Rozana and Patrick Gillogly confess that they can't get enough of vintage Chinese mijiu jars. To make each stand out, they are distributed on surfaces around the house and filled with fresh flowers.

Opposite: Marrying her Nordic heritage with her mother's advice that a home must first and foremost be cozy, Kirsten Tangeros pairs clean lines with comforting textiles and texture-rich accessories.

Art and Artisans

Whether it's a painting, music, a piece of pottery or a quilted throw, a creative expression by another person touches a part of us that we can't easily access another way. Connection, beauty, curiosity, joy...we derive so many pleasures from artworks of all kinds, so it's no wonder that we want that in our homes. Handmade objects—by you, by friends, by strangers—also lend a certain authenticity to a space, and they invite conversation. That's why any aficionado will always advise that you ask a seller for any history that they can share when you happen on a find that bears the hallmark of some kind of handcraftsmanship or other artistry. You should also scour a piece for markings or signatures to see if the internet can help; the research is useful not only for basic facts and figures but also in helping you define and develop your taste for something that already called to you organically. And then sometimes you may just enjoy indulging your imagination about who's in that amateur portrait that caught your eye.

Opposite: "I am passionate about craft; creating beauty with one's hands," says native Californian and skilled ceramicist Brian Hickman, who collects and displays all kinds of handmade pottery.

Above: Adept maker Jana Jamison works in a variety of media and appreciates others' work, such as these sculptural, handmade candlesticks offset by a religious figure holding vintage rosaries.

Right and far right: Every room of Memo Faraj's house is filled with art in some form, like this African mask. A collector of vintage frames, he offers this advice: "If you love the art but hate the frame, buy it. If you love the frame and hate the art, buy it. I collect so much of both and interchange them!"

Collections

Maybe it sparks a memory, or perhaps you simply love the shape, or the color, or the texture, but whatever it is that draws you to a particular thing—or, more likely, things—tends to leave you wanting more. From Bakelite to books to bull's-eye mirrors, collecting helps to give shape to shopping missions, be they casual or highly focused, and the collections can become useful decorating tools once you master the skill of creating meaningful and beautiful displays. For some, that could translate into grouping interesting little baubles that invite investigation when arranged under a single, eye-catching glass cloche; to others, a massed exhibit is what creates impact. The items themselves will often inform your approach, and displays can be refashioned as collections grow or change; nobody wants the feeling of living in a museum, after all. Speaking of pitfalls, to avoid having too much of a good thing, inveterate hunter-gatherers recommend digging into the history of the items you love so that you can be choosy about what makes the cut, and prioritize your collecting budget accordingly.

Opposite left: "An entire collection displayed as a whole is almost like an art piece in itself," say vintage dealers Rozana and Patrick Gillogly, whose vintage trophies are almost at capacity.

Opposite right: In a hallway, pages from an antique dictionary form a backdrop for tramp art frames, including antique thread and string frames—surely love tokens or homes for special photos, says owner Jana Jamison.

Above left: Adding to their sculpture collection has become a renewed interest for the Gilloglys, who admit that part of what dictates their displays is keeping things safely out of reach of their little ones.

Left: Although she admits that a few of her collections have outgrown her space, a true quester never quits, according to Melissa Parks, who tapped a vintage bar cart to hold McCoy pottery pieces that didn't fit in her kitchen cabinets.

Above: Included on this primitive glass and metal "table of curiosities" is a taxidermy heron, a pair of old metal shoemaker's forms, a pottery bust, a miniature diary under glass, coral and a beaver's skull, all below the watch of a dour portrait.

Self-Expression

You know you. Whatever makes you feel at home or speaks to you in a personal way is going to resonate with everyone who enters your home. Skillfully mixing and mingling your favorite colors, textures and textiles, design genres, photos and art will create spaces that are uniquely your own. "The best way to learn your style is through trial and error," says design duo Rozana and Patrick Gillogly, who truly learned by doing when they set out to furnish their first apartment, affordably. "Take your time and be open-minded," adds artist and fashion exec-turned-interior designer Memo Faraj. "I didn't develop my style overnight." Of course your budget, free time and fellow household members will factor into your design decisions too, but all our homeowners agree that it's worth holding out and making room for those things that truly fit you. "Don't fall into the trap of what's popular and trendy," cautions artist Deborah Harold. "Your home is the best way to express who you are!" Former antiques dealer Angie Cavalier couldn't agree more, noting that "The last thing the world needs is another model home."

Above left: While traveling, Memo Faraj purchased a vintage tray he intended to use for serving. After it broke in his luggage, he simply reassigned it to the wall. The mermaid mirror below was his second-ever thrifted score.

Far left: Vintage animal heads in the Gilloglys' home are representative of their two sons, since they always refer to one as a lion and the other as a bear.

Left: The vintage pineapple lamp, carved monkey and hand-painted bowl reflect Memo's taste for things that are a bit offbeat.

Opposite: A ship painting and portrait of a Royal Navy admiral pair with a blue-and-white scheme in Memo's bedroom. "I wanted to wake up to a nautical vibe," he explains.

The Homes

How do you keep a home filled with art and antiques from feeling like a museum? For this passionate collector, it comes down to creating lively displays in his Long Beach home. And then not letting them sit still for too long.

Past Present

Lifelong Southern Californian Brian Hickman favors a hands-on approach when it comes to creating things of beauty. In fact, he notes, "I am obsessed with things made by hand: old stone or lathe and plaster walls, woodblock prints, paintings, sculpture; I could watch English gardeners clip boxwood spheres and shapes all day," he says. It may be no wonder, then, that when he acquired this 1925 English cottage in the historically protected Long Beach neighborhood of Bluff Park, he put his own hands to work, planting gardens and trees outside and filling its rooms with art, found objects, handmade pottery, old wood boxes and vintage tools, among many other things that bear the mark of handcraftsmanship.

"I jokingly refer to my style either as 'high-end hoarder' or '1930s Danish artist living in exile,'" laughs Brian, although he's really more of an experimental curator. Living in an old home whose rooms open like little jewel boxes into each other, even the most interesting collectibles can quickly become clutter, and he's not a fan of the more-is-more look. Instead, he only has about a quarter of his collections on display at any given time. "I have some great cupboards in the garage that are full of things," he says. "I rotate stuff around once a year or so, because otherwise I stop appreciating it. Even the art."

Above: A mash-up of finds—a 1930s wingback chair from Craigslist, still in its original velvet; a dark oak stacked-triangle table; a brass, felt and wood table lamp —gives the living room character.

Break the Rules

Do an inspection! Turning over a floral painting purchased from Etsy revealed this moody nude on the reverse side, along with the original hanging wire, wooden shims/wedges and artist's signature.

With no need for an indoor dining room, this space was converted into a cozy reading room anchored by a vintage rug and a velvet sofa. Flea-market lighting and artworks animate the room, but its centerpiece is a planter by Swiss designer Willy Guhl, which Brian received as a gift.

"I have music playing almost 24 hours a day, so that is my greatest inspiration. In the end, what is great design but a version of jazz?"

When he's in the mood for a little change, Brian says he likes to mix it up like a dinner party. "I move stuff around and see 'who' wants to hang out, and I put them together," he says. "I might group things by shape, color or theme, or I might group them to create a story or to create tension," referring to a style mash-up he's experienced in his travels. "I'm very influenced by Italian design and the Italians' ability to live with the past and future at the same time," he says. "Sixteenth-century plasterwork with a Lucite chair? Yes. Home built as a monastery but now filled with laughter and 20 dogs and chickens running through the kitchen? Yes, please. They seem to have really captured a way of life that is very appealing. Anything goes," he observes, "as long as it creates more beauty and joy."

Spot Potential

Talk about storage furniture! This barrel-shaped vintage shipping container, still bearing an original label, has been inventively repurposed as a one-of-a-kind side table.

While he may not have the benefit of a centuries-old backdrop to work with, Brian ushers in character by way of shopping the vintage way. "About 99% of my home's contents are from flea markets and thrift stores, so they are my go-to sources," he says. One of his top quests is for vintage lighting—the new-old fixtures he has installed so far were all Etsy finds—but he keeps an eye out for his favorite collectibles, which include art, found objects and handmade pottery, to name a few. "I feel like they have stories to tell and then I get to add mine!" says Brian. Although not all stories have a happy ending: "I once carried an entire set of vintage dishes from a flea market through Italy for two weeks in a carry-on suitcase, only to have it fall off my other suitcase

Left and above: A cool all-brass table lamp highlights a mix of found wooden, metal and clay objects displayed on an old sideboard. Bearing its original distressed surface, a vintage mirror offers a perfect view of the double-sided sculpture by Matt Harward.

"About 20 years ago, I stopped worrying if something was
'the right style' and started asking if it was beautiful to me.
That changed everything!"

Above: *Natural light in the already-bright guest room is amplified by a tall Eastlake mirror. Brian added notes of color and texture with a mid-century oil painting, a sawhorse table and a vintage rug and blanket.*

in the train station on my last day and shatter into a million pieces!" he laughs. A talented ceramicist himself, these days he's looking to replace his machine-made bowls and coffee mugs with handmade pieces from artisans and is slowly building that collection.

And Brian takes a modern approach when hunting for those creations. About 20 years ago, he says, "I stopped worrying if something was 'the right style' and started asking if it was beautiful to me. That changed everything!" Admittedly, that can be easier said than done, but Brian offers a strategy.

Top: A blackened, distressed wooden hutch/ dresser is the perfect spot to display a collection of white pottery as well as everyday plates and bowls.

Above: Antique copper-clad wall-mounted shelving holds essential ingredients in glass jars, within easy reach of the modern day-starting appliances on the counter below.

The kitchen was rescued from a drab, dropped-ceiling remodel and brought back to life with vintage elements. Original beadboard and factory lighting crown the room, while an authentic, hand-painted 1950s store window promises "good food" from the vintage O'Keefe and Merritt stove/cooker.

"I love mixing old and new because otherwise you end up living in a museum and that feels like a trap."

Crafting Art-Filled Interiors

1 Trust your eye. Learn to distinguish between something you appreciate as beautiful and something you simply can't take your eyes off of. Art is oh-so-personal.

2 Reject the notion that all art is expensive. Most of Brian's pieces came from flea markets and other secondhand sources, so be patient while you build your own collection. "Beauty doesn't cost more money," Brian points out. "It just takes more time."

3 Change things up. Everything from display cabinets to gallery walls (hello, Command hooks!) will benefit from being moved around once in a while so you appreciate them in a new light.

Use your phone as a personal style guide, he says. Take a screen shot or photograph things you love from social media, blogs and your own life and adventures. "Not just interiors, but gardens, colors, textures, light and shadows," he advises. When you scroll through them, you will see an absolute pattern emerge of the colors, feelings and textures that you are attracted to over and over. It's a reliable way to help define your style and what you want around you. "If you don't see something repeated, it's not really you," he says. "I've got about 16,000 pictures on my phone and probably 1,000 or more are duplicates because I loved them enough to capture them more than once."

More than anything, though, Brian says this: "Don't be talked into someone else's version of you." When you're looking to cultivate your personal style, as long as something is well made and you are passionate about it, go for it, he says. "Life is a mash-up," he adds. "Shop accordingly!"

Above left: A colorful mid-century French lithograph, found at a flea market, reflects a white bowl from the 1960s.

Opposite: A gallery wall covered with flea-market art and objects, as well as a wooden tribal mask, enriches the office. More sculptural pieces, including a 1950s marble lamp and matte-green pottery from the 1920s, continue the artful theme.

Left and below: The other side of Brian's office features a collection of found paintings, woodblocks, prints and sketches. Collected ceramic and glass jars hold pens, brushes and vintage sculpture tools on the 1920s dining table, which he uses as a desk.

Opposite: Under a canopy of sycamores, a vintage farm table is topped with a linen featherbed cover used as a tablecloth and set with a collection of handmade dishes. This is Brian's favorite "room," as it reminds him of his travels in Italy.

As this cute California cottage closes in on its 100th birthday, its vintage-loving owners eschewed cosmetic changes in favor of appointing rooms with eye-catching pieces that reflect a sentimental journey.

Modern Family

It started organically enough: As newlyweds, Rozana and Patrick Gillogly were looking to outfit their first apartment affordably, which sent them into the secondhand market. But the design-loving duo discovered they had a knack for picking out the good stuff, and thus a business was born, now over a decade ago. The San Pedro, California, natives search for and sell their wares all over the country, at markets and online at throughtheportholeshop.com. About five years ago, the couple decided to put down permanent roots in a neighborhood with a small-town vibe, which was anchored in their purchase of this charming Craftsman cottage. Although small on square footage, the home was just right for their needs, featuring a plan that flows perfectly for entertaining and built-in character to spare. "We haven't done much besides painting and changing some fixtures," Rozana says. "We love our small house because it's all that we need. It's the perfect size for our little family and great for having guests over, and really fun to decorate."

And she means that in the present tense, because it's an ongoing process. "Our style is really eclectic and ever-evolving," notes Rozana. For these self-professed design-lovers, outfitting their home has been something of a labor of love, as they've carefully chosen each furniture item and accessory—from a TV console that had to be carried down a hill and through multiple staircases, to shapely figures and sculptures—that has come through the door.

Left and above: In the living room, prize finds include a black spotlight sourced on a trip through Arkansas and a "tooth ottoman" picked up at a flea market. Patrick bought the classical guitar in high school, and beside hangs his grandfather's guitar from the 1970s.

"We love the story behind the pieces," Rozana explains. "We can tell you the 'who, what and where' about almost everything in the house. Our rule is that we have to love it before we bring it home."

That doesn't mean anything is too precious, though. While Rozana and Patrick enjoy fine design, it has to come with a sense of real life—especially since they have added two boys to the household since moving in. "Having little ones has definitely changed how we select furniture and accessories for our home," Rozana admits. "We've learned to choose more functional pieces that help us organize and declutter. Plus most of our collections have moved high out of the reach of the baby," she adds.

Above and opposite: The vintage medical cabinet was a business purchase, but proved too beautiful to sell. It houses, among other favorite things, overflow from the mantel's trophy display, an antique French mannequin and a brass date display that's permanently set to the couple's anniversary.

Make It Personal

Set up rooms for how you really live. Rozana says their coffee maker gets a lot of use, so they crafted an ad hoc coffee bar on top of an old workbench. The vintage German breadboard nearby doubles as a charcuterie platter and hanging art.

Those collections include an impressive array of vintage trophies—"We haven't been able to stop buying trophies yet, but we're running out of space to put them, so I suppose that will be our stopping point," Rozana muses—and they're always on the hunt for figures, sculptures and busts. Once home, those prize finds are displayed en masse. "A collection displayed as a whole is almost like an art piece in itself," notes Rozana, whose current challenge is finding wall art for the boys' space. "Their room is always changing and adapting as they grow," she says, adding that she and Patrick enjoy having something specific to hunt for while they're shopping for their business.

Indeed, being in the business, they follow the advice they offer to anyone trying to cultivate a style: "Go with your gut, and don't be afraid to experiment.

"We have always had a love and passion for vintage furniture, which is never perfect. We believe the perfect home is comfortable, laid-back, functional and beautiful."

How To Shop Like a Pro

1 What's Rozana and Patrick's number one rule when they're on the hunt? "Buy the good stuff when you see it," they say, "because chances are when you are specifically looking for it, you won't be able to get your hands on it."

2 Speaking of good stuff, if there's a particular category you love—English pottery, mid-century furniture, antique quilts—it pays to do advance and ongoing research so that you're able to identify a gem on the spot.

3 There's an art to negotiating a price, but being courteous to the vendor and showing interest in an item's history are always welcome icebreakers.

Left: In their bedroom, Patrick fashioned the Swiss cross piece that sits over a narrow vintage elm bench by stitching vintage indigo to an old piece of canvas.

Giant wallpaper screen prints from an old factory make colorful, textural wall art. Antique convex Federal mirrors are always keepers for this treasure-hunting duo; this is one of their two favorites.

The best way to learn is through trial and error," the couple says. (One major error to avoid, though: Not knowing the measurements of your walls and doorways before buying, especially when it comes to antique pieces that may have unusual dimensions or are one-of-a-kind and not returnable—"We learned that the hard way," jokes Rozana.)

For this duo, the tie that binds is good design, regardless of whether a piece is old, new or somewhere in between. They love the textures of leather and wood that bear the patina of use, and value the imperfections that come along with decorating the vintage way. "We have fun with our style, keep it casual, and don't take it too seriously," Rozana says. "We believe the perfect home is comfortable, laid-back, functional and beautiful."

Have Fun

Don't take your décor too seriously. When the Gilloglys commandeered this distressed black console for a diaper-changing station, they also found the perfect spot for their vintage "No Dumping" sign.

Opposite and above: The entryway's cabinet offers a pop of gray-blue color and a spot to stash absolutely everything from a dog leash to spare candles. The framed boat flags on the wall pay homage to their oceanside location, and the pair's favorite chippy-paint "David" bust sits below. A full-size, but much smaller, David is dwarfed by a brass necklace that their three-year-old son refused to leave behind at an estate sale.

Artist Deborah Harold is a lifelong California girl, and every inch of the home she shares with her partner exemplifies a relaxed SoCal vibe. The pair found their tiny cottage—nestled atop a canyon and overlooking both a creek and the ocean—12 years ago and instantly fell in love. Says Deborah, "It's like living in a tree house!"

Nesting Instincts

While its now-expanded footprint has grown the house to a still-cozy 1,700 sq ft/158sq m, it feels much larger, owing both to Deborah's design style and what she refers to as the home's "effortless indoor-outdoor feeling," which is a big part of what initially attracted her and her partner Clyde Harkins to the 1950s coastal cottage. There is a large deck—one of the improvements the couple made over the years—great for relaxing, enjoying meals and taking in views of the water. And, notes Deborah, "The home is situated in such a way that we can enjoy both the sunrise and sunset."

"A collected and curated home is what I've strived for always
—not falling into the trap of what's popular and trendy."

Opposite and above: *The living room is an eclectic mix of pieces Deborah has collected over the years. "I have a hard time passing up an old pottery piece or silver dome," she notes. Open to the kitchen, the room is a hangout for watching TV and enjoying a fire.*

In keeping with the lovely views and wonderful flow—an open concept, with four different French doors leading out to the deck—Deborah's design also visually expands the space, beautifully. Not to mention simply. "The small size of our home has caused me to just use what I love. I go for uncluttered décor, as [a space] can feel really small with too many 'things,'" says the former interior designer, who now devotes herself to fine art (you can see some of her work at deborahharold.com).

Not surprisingly, Deborah thinks of decorating in terms of art, explaining why she always chooses white as her go-to for walls and upholstery: "It's like starting with a blank canvas; you can then go in any direction with interesting art, books, lamps and textiles." It's an approach that has served her well in the past too. "My style has pretty much stayed the same over the years," Deborah says. "I'm a very casual person, so my interiors reflect that."

Effortless Indoor-Outdoor Living

1 Double down on durability. Count on tough surfaces like stone and hardwood floors to stand up to high traffic while also being easy to clean. Scatter mats and small area rugs soften the look and catch dirt.

2 Make the transition seamless. Inside, include abundant natural texture and woven furnishings that echo those used outdoors; outside, count on weatherproof fabrics to add comfort and color.

3 Invest in your entryways. Window walls with folding and/ or retractable doors, double French doors and deluxe, extra-wide sliders will pay off in the long run for their beauty and ease of daily use.

Above and above right: Embellished with pieces from here and there, the remodeled kitchen is a source of daily joy for Deborah, who keeps a lamp on the counter, as it often doubles as her office space. To unplug, the family heads outside to enjoy a daily dose of nature among mature sycamores.

In the case of Deborah's house, "casual" means welcoming and relaxing— never boring. Large, sink-into, white denim slipcovered chairs are offset with antique furniture that, she says, "isn't fussy or fragile. The antiques are a nice contrast to the crisp white overstuffed furniture. Pillows in ethnic fabrics are where I like a pop of color and texture. I use trays, stacks of books and fresh flowers in simple vessels to add beauty and bring nature inside."

Natural materials play a key role in Deborah's design strategy as well. Sisal rugs, a mixture of woods and muted tones enhance the indoor-outdoor feel and let her beloved collectibles—as well as her own artwork—really take center stage. In fact, her favorite decorating tip is to mix contemporary art with antiques. "They complement one another with the stark contrast," she notes. While Deborah says she likes anything with a history ("It makes a home so much more interesting"), she is partial to vintage silver pieces...and maybe a few other things too: "I also collect vintage fabrics, from my travels to Turkey, Vietnam, France and Peru, that I drape over my white furniture or stack together in a bookcase to display. Baskets also bring a warmth to the home and are so useful and lovely."

Opposite: "We love every room in our house and use every room," says Deborah. Accordingly, denim slipcovers stand up to traffic—and regular naps for labs Lena and Bodhi—in the sitting room. An old bookcase holds her art and design books.

Have Fun

Don't be too precious with well-loved accessories. A footed porcelain bowl that belonged to Deborah's grandmother has a tiny chip, but the dogs don't mind—they appreciate the elevated drinking station.

"The small size of our home has caused me to just use what I love."

"I am partial to anything with a history. It makes a home so much more interesting."

Her decorate-with-what-you-love technique, as well as the genuine appreciation and affection Deborah has for each item, is what gives her home such personality and such a lived-in feel. "My style is relaxed, eclectic and imperfect," Deborah explains, "but my design advice to anyone would be to make your home your own. Make it personal. A collected and curated home is what I've strived for always—not falling into the trap of what's popular and trendy. And your home is the best way to express who you are!"

Spot Potential

It can be unwise to collect for the sake of collecting, but buying vintage and antique storage pieces is a safe bet, as they are useful in every room, like this armoire Deborah picked up at an antiques shop.

A big part of the cottage's charm is its indoor-outdoor feel, which is enhanced by white walls and lots of glass. Wood accents and accessories in neutral tones support the natural vibe.

This homeowner is proud of her Norwegian heritage, and it informs every aspect of her design style. But don't expect to find a white palette and minimal furnishings when you step into her charming Cape Cod just outside Chicago.

Welcome Home

"I've always wanted my home to reflect warmth and comfort," says Kirsten Tangeros. Growing up, her Norwegian-born mom would say, " 'You have to make it cozy,' and I feel like that has been the driving influence of my style," she says. And how, exactly, does Kirsten define cozy? She aims for a collected-over-time look, citing country homes in Europe as inspiration. "Anywhere that features old rugs, paintings, textiles, books and 'settle-in' furniture is perfect!" she explains.

When Kirsten and her husband, Chris Thomas, moved into their 1940s hideaway 23 years ago, they were only the second family to live there, so they knew changes had to be made. But Kirsten had grown up in a Cape Cod and loved the nooks and crannies inherent in that architectural style. "The rooms are a bit small, but I love that it forces togetherness as a family," she says.

Opposite: Hand-painted using the traditional Norwegian folk art of rosemaling, the eat-in kitchen's corner hutch/dresser holds family antiques as well as thrift finds from, notes Kirsten, "Norway's version of Goodwill."

Above left: When a family friend was selling her pine dining-room set from Norway, Kirsten jumped at the chance to buy it, recalling that it evoked memories of "vacationing in the Norwegian mountains."

Above right: The kitchen underwent an update after the couple moved in. The island was a $200 find at a nearby flea market, while the $16 painted stepstool adds that pop of color Kirsten loves—and it comes in handy too.

"The rooms are a bit small, but I love that it forces togetherness as a family."

In keeping, Kirsten teases that what initially drew her to embrace not-all-brand-new style was having a husband, kids and dogs. "I want to use the things in my home that I've surrounded myself with. Those things that are old and used and imperfect are often the most beautiful of all."

But arriving at that "lived-in" attitude was an evolution. Kirsten says she and a friend always laugh together about the "style checklist" they used to have: a rose painting, a McCoy pot, white ironstone, a chandelier…"All of those things are wonderful and interesting," she notes. "But I've come to realize that my house doesn't need to be all Shabby Chic or Boho.

Below and bottom: Just some of the charming vignettes that add interest to the living room: a bowl filled with "dog doo-dads," as Kirsten calls them, and two flea-market trunks—one featuring folk art painting, the other faded wallpaper.

The gallery wall in the living room showcases Kirsten's love of collecting old paintings; two of her favorite subjects are dogs and white farmhouses.

"Those things that are old and used and imperfect are often the most beautiful of all."

Right: The wall of the staircase—painted in Farrow & Ball's "Lichen" in a nod to English country style—displays just some of Kirsten's extensive collection of dog paintings.

My house can have elements of everything I love, and that's what will make it interesting and [reflect] me. I don't need to fall into a category; that's why I love the styles that look like they've evolved over time," she explains.

That said, Kirsten enjoys mixing in new items alongside old treasures. Sometimes new just makes sense in terms of functionality and practicality, she says. "And sometimes you need to think about other family members.

Below: Every corner in the Tangeros house features an eye-catching item. "I'm always up for an antiquing road trip, and I always like to bring home something unique from my travels," says Kirsten.

Have Fun

Collectibles on the small side are impactful when displayed en masse. If they start to outgrow your space, take a page from Kirsten's book and try to limit any additions to specific colors or makers.

Just because I love old things doesn't mean my kids want to be surrounded by them all the time!"

Hopefully her kids (and her husband, and their three rescue dogs, and two turtles) love dog paraphernalia, though, because Kirsten's biggest collections are canine figurines and paintings, and they can be found in almost every room.

Make It *Koselig* (aka Cozy)

1 Incorporating handiwork, like the traditional folk art of rosemaling, lends authenticity and comfort to a space because you know someone's personal touch and time were intended to embellish and beautify a space before you got there.

2 Layer textiles. Whether it's sheepskin over sisal, quilted fabric thrown over a sofa or a wonderful wool blanket adding warmth atop a well-worn linen sheet, there's something sumptuous about that extra layer.

3 Fill in the blanks. Cluttered surfaces are the opposite of relaxing, but walls filled with interesting artwork and pictures and intentional displays of beloved objects answer questions about the residents in a way that makes guests feel at home.

Left: The office/sitting room holds more family treasures—including a chair that originally belonged to Kirsten's grandparents. "I love to incorporate elements of my heritage into my home," she says.

Opposite: In the mudroom, a striking antique hand-painted Dutch-Indonesian cabinet stores piles of vintage textiles; the family added the larger space onto the house after they moved in.

Above: This quiet corner of the master bedroom spotlights Scandinavian art. One piece is a Finnish painting Kirsten found for $5 at a neighbor's garage sale; the other features Norwegian fjords.

Right: Even the bathroom is bathed in vintage textiles. The shower curtain (which Kirsten got for $10) actually started life as an embroidered tablecloth.

Try though she might, Kirsten has a tough time editing herself. "It's hard," she notes, "because they all make the cut with their sweet faces."

But she's just staying true to her own decorating advice: "If it speaks to you, grab it. Trust your gut. All that matters is that you like it. Your home will only truly feel like home when it reflects you. When you follow a trend, you just look and feel like everyone else."

Make It Personal

Connect to your heritage. For Kirsten, that was brought home when she found on Facebook a headboard and dresser hand-painted by none other than Per Lysne, the Norwegian folk artist who brought rosemaling to the U.S.

Limited square footage is, well, limiting. But according to this Chicago-area visionary, her home's small size provided her with a crash course in home decorating. "It has forced me to be more creative with how I display my collections, and to think about how to create continuity and cohesion from room to room since everything is connected," she says. "It has forced me to learn how to edit."

Opposite: Guests are greeted by Liberty of London fabric covering an antique Craftsman-style bench. Melissa made a savvy swap to score the pricey hand-painted antique tri-fold screen behind it.

Above: Melissa collects peacocks, so when she spotted this brass peacock vase for $14 at a Nebraska antiques mall, it was a no-brainer. She fills it weekly with flowers from her garden to brighten her office.

Out of the Ordinary

"It's not a fancy house," says writer and vintage dealer Melissa Parks of her and her family's diminutive 1920s bungalow. But the what-they-could-afford-at-the-time abode purchased over 20 years ago ticked an important box: it wasn't new. "I wanted hardwood floors, crown molding/cornicing and to imagine the lives of those who lived here before," she says. Forging a future by embracing the past has in fact been a lifelong habit of hers, fueled in large part by a dislike of following trends. As a teen, Melissa went headlong into the thrift-shop world to build a wardrobe that wasn't like anyone else's.

Left: *The Victorian-era piano was a Craigslist find that Melissa plays regularly enough to merit its floor space. It performs double duty as a mantel, and a mid-century gilt bench below ($7 at Goodwill!) brightens the scene.*

Below: *Part of Melissa's white McCoy pottery collection nestles atop a primitive cabinet built in the 1800s, long before the TV it houses. The chinoiserie chair in front of it was a thrift-shop find.*

Right: *It was a worthwhile expense to have an upholsterer rebuild the frame and cover the living-room sofa, which Melissa found free on Facebook Marketplace. Antique silk peacock screen panels above it accentuate the room's height.*

And that's how she decorates today. "I want my home to singularly reflect who I am," she says. "I want to live with items that I never want to throw away because they are meaningful; not just placeholders."

For Melissa, who is a gifted storyteller, that meaning is derived from searching for pieces that also come with a story, whether it's one she knows or simply imagines. Flea markets and consignment stores are therefore her shopping haunts, as their wares can fill a room, literally and figuratively, with history. If she picks up a portrait, for example, she loves to wonder who is pictured, and who the artist might have been. That thrift-store table? Melissa likes to ponder who might have eaten around it before it was discarded.

Left: Anchoring her gallery of water lily paintings is an ornate antique corner chair. Melissa spotted it when a vendor was packing up in the rain and therefore willing to part with it for $20.

Below: Next to the sofa, the Italian gilt marble-topped vitrine was a $20 Goodwill find that now houses alabaster birdbaths and white beaded flowers. Above it, a lotus wall sconce bought in Chicago was eventually outfitted with antique silk shades found six years later in Minneapolis.

Opposite: A $10 Italian marble table that was stripped of shellac and resealed is now the star of the dining area. Campaign-style chairs priced at $4 apiece surround it and a refinished curbside-find cabinet supports antique Florentine mirrors.

"My home has a moody, artistic and, at times, romantic feel. I gravitate towards whimsy."

Editing Matters in a Small Home

1 If you're a collector, accept that you can't show everything at once. "I've had to figure out a way to rein in my collections through grouping, and using cabinets as vignette opportunities," notes Melissa.

2 The more floor space you see, the bigger a room looks, so it's important to make smart use of vertical displays. Hang artwork to accentuate ceiling height, and consider built-in shelving to make a place for everything and keep furniture surfaces clear.

3 Get choosy. Before anything even comes home, Melissa now limits herself to the least-flawed or best version of a wish-list item.

Opposite: A pretty textile covers what's actually a pullout sofa in Melissa's office so that the space can double as a guest room. Her husband built the surrounding cabinet to hold her ever-expanding collections.

Above right: A majolica jardinière holds vintage and antique French beaded flowers that Melissa has been collecting for more than 20 years now. Just one stem can cost up to $20, so she muses that this is now a pricey bouquet!

"I like to imagine the story behind antiques. What compelled someone to thread hundreds of tiny beads on wire to create a beaded flower?"

But any wistfulness is matched by practicality; Melissa appreciates that secondhand shopping is easier on the wallet and is more sustainable than buying new. "It also allows for individuality and demands an artistic sensibility to pull it all together," she adds.

Citing influences like designer John Derian and the Bloomsbury Group, Melissa has learned the art of mixing and matching antiques and layering in objects of interest to create a rich effect. In her dining room, for example, she has a 1980s Italian marble table—a $10 score that turned out to be a designer piece worth thousands—paired with a turn-of-the-century industrial cabinet, a 1920s light fixture and gilt mirrors. "It's the unexpected mix that delights the eye and keeps it from looking like a museum or period house," she notes. Not that they haven't worked to give the house authentic character. Over the years, she and her husband have redone the floors, gutted bathrooms to add features like a clawfoot tub and pedestal sinks, and overhauled the kitchen. All the lighting is now antique too.

But it's the finishing touches that get Melissa's heart racing. Collections, which include McCoy pottery, beadwork, folk art, mirrors, paintings and

Set up your surroundings for daily inspiration. For Melissa, waking up to this seascape wall transports her to the Oregon coast, which is her favorite place in the world.

Opposite: Gold leafing fronts each of the drawers on a hand-painted piece that Melissa coveted for years. Over it, a rare Italian micro-mosaic mirror nestles above a snaking bottle-cap chain.

Left and below: In the bedroom, a seascape gallery wall emerges around an antique-framed mirror, which is actually a two-way glass that hides a TV. You wouldn't guess that the antique bed is brass because its spindles are covered in mother-of-pearl.

other artworks, are displayed together as an installation or mixed up but unified by color and texture. Moody blue and green walls provide the backdrop for accents tinged with brassy gold that feel European, Melissa says, adding that a home should reflect those who live in it—their history, their passions and interests, and the memories that create warmth. "I think that's why I obsess over the Bloomsbury Group's Charleston Farmhouse. Fireplaces were painted, portraits of family members hung throughout the house, garden flowers were tossed into handmade vases, throws draped over furniture—all of it reflective of the artists who lived there. It is casual but sumptuous," she says. "And definitely not cookie-cutter."

Spot Potential

Reimagine your floor plan for how you really live. While Melissa and her husband forfeited a closet/cupboard, it doubled their bathroom's size and made space for an antique clawfoot tub.

Opposite: Melissa's collection of green McCoy pottery is shown off thanks to cabinets that didn't quite get finished with doors during a remodel. Crowning the kitchen is a Feldman Lotus brass chandelier (with matching pendants), a room-making $150 score from a Puget Sound flea market.

Above and right: To cope with Chicago's long, cold winters, an antique tub from a Chicago salvage yard that Melissa's husband refinished was a must-have addition to their bathroom. A new-old pedestal sink echoes the look.

After a day trip north of Chicago, a couple unexpectedly found themselves trotting down a virtual path to discover what was once a horse barn that played host to events for the rich and famous. "This home has a literal soul," they say. "When you walk in, you can feel it."

Blue Ribbon Reno

Pandemic living closed in on everyone, and, with two active young boys in a small city house, Molly and Nate Kipp were feeling the squeeze. Looking for a little relief, they headed to the historic suburb of Lake Forest, Illinois, known for its nature preserves and lovely homes. So charmed by their afternoon bike ride through the area that they returned the very next day, the pair then found themselves going down a digital real-estate rabbit hole that night. They clicked on The Polo House.

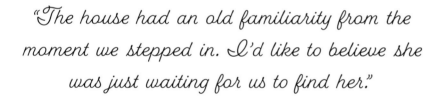

"The house had an old familiarity from the moment we stepped in. I'd like to believe she was just waiting for us to find her."

Built in 1939 as a horse barn on a 20-acre/8-hectare farm owned by the Carney family, who hosted casual polo matches and lively dinners (some right in the stables!) for well-heeled friends and American notables like Henry Ford and the Kennedy family, the barn had been converted into a family home in 1978. "Always suckers for a house with a story, we decided to take a look at it just for fun," says Molly. "I had low expectations, as it had been on the market for well over a year, but when I walked inside my heart raced and my breath caught. It was old and squeaky and had water damage on the ceilings, but it just immediately felt like home." They hadn't planned on moving...but they were hooked.

And luckily the couple knew exactly what they were getting into with their new home. "It's lived up to our expectations of being a relative money pit, but it's honestly a privilege to honor her with updates," notes Molly.

Spot Potential

When the bones are good,
a piece can be restored. The
brass hardware on this
shelving caught Molly's eye;
the wood just needed love.
Turns out it had been a
display table from the
original Marshall Field's.

Left: A local craftsman—cost-efficiently, Molly
notes—fabricated the furniture to fit the size
and scale of this great room, where the family
gathers to watch movies. "To honor the home's
history but not in a gratuitous way," Molly says,
"the chairs feature horse tack 'belts.'"

They've replaced what were five different types of flooring downstairs with a uniform white oak herringbone, are installing custom wood windows, updated an upstairs bathroom and plan a full kitchen reno down the line, all with an eye to honoring the home's history. Getting rained on—inside—the first night in the house also meant a new roof went on five years earlier than expected. But the investments relate less to resale and more to use value. "I'm passionate about creating a home that my kids can't wait to come home to, where we create memories and where we welcome others to come in and stay awhile," Molly says.

Accordingly, creature comforts come by way of inviting, organic textures, from soft wool and linen to rugged marble, stone and clay. "Being a well-lived-in home, texture helps hide the impact of young boys," notes Molly, who relies on fluffy wool rugs to blur footprints, nubby bouclé to conceal sticky finger goop and Mongolian sheepskin that is basically impenetrable, she says. "Our family room has a white couch that has been trashed by the kids," she adds, thinking that a few white hemp rugs might be its next covering. "But it's a couch. It's meant to get used. And worn."

"To me, beauty without imperfection is boring. I'm more into décor with a bit of grit, quirk, patina and weirdness."

Opposite: *Molly and Nate purchased the Hungarian workbench from the former homeowners and topped it with one of her prize Facebook finds: a 6-ft/1.8m mirror (the hayloft overlooks this space, which has 28-ft/8.5m ceilings). Artists created the European-looking ombre limewashed walls.*

Right: *Giant cloches on the workbench contain a sculptural wasp nest and a collection of horse bones found during a nearby excavation. "We assume the horse died of natural causes and had been buried," Molly laughs, noting that no horses were harmed for the display!*

A Case for Customizing

1 Finding great secondhand furniture for next to nothing leaves room in the budget for upgrades. Funky side chairs Molly found now look luscious covered in mohair, and a local artist transformed an armoire that cost $130 with an ebonized finish and glass inserts.

2 If you need shelving for an odd nook or a sofa that fits your space exactly, having those pieces made by a local craftsperson may cost about the same as retail and pays off in being exactly right.

3 Looking at paint swatches but nothing's quite right? If there's a color you love or want to match, work with a good paint shop to mix it up to your specifications.

Have Fun

Sometimes you have to buy now, figure it out later. That's what Molly did when she spied these tin chocolate mold "tiles" used for the Detroit Tigers concessions. Years later, they adorn her son Augie's room.

Opposite: Fully enveloped in cedar and sporting vintage portraits, the cozy tack room is one of Molly's favorite spaces. "I wanted the room to have a Ralph Lauren vibe; it's the one room in the house where I unashamedly embraced the equestrian," she confesses.

Molly readily admits, though, that a big part of her laid-back attitude comes from sourcing most of her furniture on Facebook Marketplace. That couch? $90. "It's a Henredon, incredibly well made—it'll last for generations—and I had it recovered for a couple hundred bucks," Molly says. "It feels good to me to reuse and upcycle an heirloom piece; it was saved from a landfill.

Above and right: The master bedroom resides in the barn's former hayloft, complete with original floors and now-nailed-shut doors for pitching hay downstairs. Molly plans to sand the beams back to their original raw wood to tone with the moody peacock-blue paint she chose to work with the room's lack of natural light. A vintage rug "won for a song" at auction, animal-print stools and flea-market seascapes lend a sense of well-traveled adventure to the nest.

I also saved a ton of cash and I was able to help support a local artisan—a win-win-win." As a child of an inveterate antiques-shop-lover (and deal-getter), it may be no surprise that Molly values personality and patina over the spit-and-polish of something new, unless it was made by an artist or craftsperson. "This was a home to horses. I don't want it to ever feel frivolous or pretentious," Molly says. "The ceilings are low, the plaster is crumbly, many of the walls are simply cedar. My hope is that the home feels down-to-earth and one-of-a-kind, all at once, because that's what she was made to be."

Above: The walls of son Oliver's room come to vivid life thanks to "Battle of Valmy" wallpaper from Brunschwig & Fils. Atop the dresser are vintage French toy finds.

Opposite: Molly designed the bed and desk and had her furniture maker build them to fit the space, but otherwise relied on almost all vintage sources to make the room complete.

THE CAMERON COLLECTION   Colin Ford

Forget any preconceived notions that live-work spaces are cramped or charmless. "It's lofty and bright with a layout that's open plan but still retains enclosures for a cozy feeling," says this Chicago prop stylist of the apartment she renovated above a studio she rents out for shoots.

Industrial Evolution

Opposite: Johanna had this letter-size print of her mother's foot enlarged and framed. "I love its graphic nature contrasted with the deeply personal image," she says. The plant pot in front of it was made by her mother in the 1980s.

Above right: Light floods in through windows at either end of the apartment, and this cozy window seat in the dining room provides a spot to sit and read or scope out what's happening on the street below.

Finding and renovating rundown properties was a hobby stylist Johanna Brannan Lowe had long before flipping became fashionable. But she took things to a new level, literally, with her latest residence, which sits above a photo studio she created and owns in a 125-ish-year-old commercial building in the artsy Logan Square district. "These old storefront buildings help preserve the density that makes for walkable, vibrant urban neighborhoods, such as mine," Johanna says, noting that she's surrounded by independent businesses who all support each other and is spoiled for choice when it comes to bars and restaurants. So the location made the effort (translation: gut renovation) of her second-floor nest worthwhile.

After she had all-new plumbing and electric, as well as radiant floor heat— open, industrial space plus Chicago winters make this an understandable

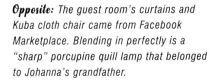

Opposite: The guest room's curtains and Kuba cloth chair came from Facebook Marketplace. Blending in perfectly is a "sharp" porcupine quill lamp that belonged to Johanna's grandfather.

Above: "The long, skinny guest bedroom enabled me to create two rooms in one; a big cozy bed and then a desk and sitting area that can function off the dining room as an office," Johanna explains.

luxury—and new windows and extra-tall doors installed, the fun part started. "I love to make my homes look like I have lived in them for years by layering found items that create a comfortable, lived-in feel," she says. So she goes out of her way to "buy old" as much as possible, without spending a mint.

"I have been on a quest for these things since I used to help my mother in a charity shop when I was a five-year-old," Johanna says of her childhood in London, England. "We used to sort through all the donations to put them up for sale. At that time my main focus was the 1950's netted frou-frou dresses

Below: Part of the living room includes treasures brought along from Johanna's life in Michigan, including a blue chippy-paint sideboard, an oculus mirror and a tall 1920s mirror that came out of her old farmhouse.

Opposite: The living area is made flexible with the addition of easy-to-move-around cabriole-leg chairs from Marshall Field's that Joanna scored secondhand from Instagram and had reupholstered. The copper-top table was another London import.

Above: A dining table that belonged to Mies van der Rohe's grandson is surrounded by chairs featuring Johanna's favorite textures of well-worn wood and a bit of fluffy sheepskin. In the foreground, her mother's cast-iron plant stand holds a collection of mortars and pestles.

in magical jewel tones, and then I progressed from there to jewelry and then homewares and furniture." Her love affair with vintage is both long-standing and relatable to kindred souls: she loves things that are unique. "You know you can't easily go and find another one, and every imperfection in them only adds to that charm," she observes. "Large turkey platters from the early Victorian era studded with steel staples and still perfectly functional, for instance; that object meant a lot to them and it does to me 150 years later."

Her new-old loft is filled with many personally meaningful things. Much of the furniture came from her mother's home in England. After she passed away in 2018, Johanna shipped all of her favorite pieces over, including the

Comfortable but Not Cluttered

1 Whether they're family heirlooms or prize finds, vintage items impart a singular warmth to a home, but too many of them will overwhelm the eye and the spirit, which ruins the effect. Be disciplined: "Do not turn one well-chosen object into a collection, or collect for collecting's sake," Johanna advises. "Love what you are buying."

2 Look for pieces you won't be scared to actually use. You may find a tray that's pretty enough to hang on a wall, but you'll enjoy it all the more if you can grab it for serving drinks or dessert when the time comes.

3 Leave some breathing space. You can add layers of richness and texture in every room, but balance it with moments of blank space.

giant gilded mirror that provided "a very stressful moment" when it came time to unpack the crate. She also took a chance on shipping marble slabs that had lived on her mother's balcony. Honed and installed to fashion a marble sink and counter, it's now the feature she loves most in her bathroom. And then there's her dining table, which she bought from Alan Robandt, a good friend and antiques dealer in Michigan. "He told me it belonged to Mies van der Rohe's grandson and it just so happens I am acquainted with him and his wife," says Johanna. "The table was used by them for many years and many entertaining events. It's super to have it still be in the family, so to speak."

Break the Rules

Don't be afraid to make ad hoc adjustments to furniture. While renovating, Johanna added wheels to her marble-topped table so that she could move it around easily, but now she loves it this way.

Above: "I never considered my taste to be particularly feminine until I decided to do a pink plaster treatment on the wall," says Johanna of her romantic kitchen. The effect is helped along by the crystal chandelier.

Opposite: A painted and decoupaged toolbox caddy holds "a mostly useless collection of objects I just really like," says Johanna. That includes British tea bags and a pie bird and egg timer from her childhood.

Integrating her favorite items into her décor is a practice Johanna relies on for creating a functional and interesting home. Not one to display collections—which she keeps to a minimum to thwart any temptation to hoard, though she readily admits that she's "a sucker for a beautiful heavy linen sheet, preferably with an embroidered initial to know how loved it was by someone in the past"—she instead makes use of all her treasured possessions in everyday life. "Art and handmade, vintage and new, they all should be able to mingle," Johanna says, adding, "It's just how you find the way to do it effortlessly."

Opposite: In the simple and serene bedroom, a painted twig table from Michigan cozies up to a bed topped with sumptuous linen and an antique door curtain as a throw.

Left: Johanna took a chance on shipping two marble slabs that sat on her mother's London balcony. They arrived intact, honed up beautifully and combine to create a unique vanity. It's illuminated in part by wall sconces that Johanna fashioned herself from industrial stamped metal cylinders.

Above: A vintage Spanish leather stool that belonged to Johanna's grandfather makes a handsome perch under the American of Martinsville dresser she found on Facebook.

"I love to make my homes look like I have lived in them for years by layering found items that create a comfortable, lived-in feel."

"Nothing is precious, even though most of my décor is irreplaceable," says this Dallas homeowner of her tasteful and interesting array of never-new furniture and accessories. And that sets the stage for a home designed to be sustainable, creative and inviting...while not taking itself too seriously.

Urban Renewal

Opposite: *"I collect books and masks and art, and it all seems to end up in the office area," says Kaitlyn, noting that her favorite mask is the white vintage Mexican one, which was a gift from her husband.*

Above right: *Another mask and a gilded wooden mirror scored from an estate sale overlook a thrift-shop table in the dining room. Raleigh, the family's Sussex spaniel, loves the window-side nap zone.*

"The neighborhood, the exterior, the trees and the fact that a flipper hadn't gotten to it yet and it had its charm intact." That's what homeowners Kaitlyn Coffee and husband Nate say motivated them to purchase this mid-century ranch. The former owner, a vintage dealer, had lived there for 50 years, so while some updates were necessary to bring the home into the current century, all the renovations—kitchen, master bedroom, all-new flooring and windows—were carried out with an eye to matching what someone may have done in 1963, when the house was built.

But don't mistake it for a strict restoration. Although Kaitlyn sourced lots of low-profile Italian mid-century furniture, wood, chrome and stone— "I really like to imagine this is a house built in Italy in the 1960s that someone has lived in for 40 years," she confesses—her driving force is simple. "I am passionate about using secondhand, vintage and antique items to create a comfortable, casual and interesting home," she says. A trained graphic designer who has built a business on creative endeavors from art direction to home styling, she describes her style as collected, folky, art-forward, colorful and cinematic, citing movies and set design from the 1980s as one of her biggest influences. "I am passionate about vintage art and objects, the stories they tell and the conversations they spark," she adds. And that's reflected in her home because, with very few exceptions, every single item is secondhand.

Like many kindred vintage-loving spirits, she comes by it honestly. Every weekend, she and her dad would hit Dallas-area estate sales and collect treasures. "I loved, loved, loved being inside someone else's house," she says. "Seeing how they lived, what they loved and collected, what books they read...I got the bug really early." But she has a grown-up incentive to keep the habit: "I like that when you buy vintage and antique items you aren't participating in the type of capitalism that is detrimental to our world."

"I love when people gift me things that I really love. It shows that they see me!"

Make It Personal

Leave room for mementos. Kaitlyn keeps little notes from clients and friends in her work area to remind her of the kind things they've said to her.

The dining set from Nate's grandmother—"The coolest lady alive!" says Kaitlyn—roots the room in family history. Spotted at a garage sale, the ostrich painting always fetches lots of likes on social media.

Spot Potential

It pays off to go beyond the extra mile for a prize find, like this extremely heavy yet also fragile—and very hard to move—table carved from one single tree.

Opposite and below: Found on eBay, a Picasso exhibition poster from the Montreal Museum of Art presides over cool new terrazzo countertops and groovy vintage oak counter stools in the revamped kitchen. A window ledge above the sink shows off a few of Kaitlyn's favorite thrifted whatnots.

Plus, she adds, "I like that the items find you; you don't just go to a store and pick what they have in stock that all your neighbors have too."

Those neighbors wouldn't have her "bone" table, for example, so named because the all-cut-from-one-tree piece is painted a glossy white such that its branches bear an uncanny skeletal resemblance. According to the seller, it came from the Southern Methodist University Library when they were remodeling in the 1960s or '70s. "I guess they had a sale and no one bought it because it weighs like 1,000 pounds [454kg] and is really awkward to move. I somehow got it in my car and into our house using a dolly," says Kaitlyn,

"Don't buy something because someone else tells you that it's cool."

Cultivating Personal Style

1 Focus on what moves you. It could be travel, a relative's home, walks in nature...it's up to you to define. "My biggest influences are movies and set design from the 1980s, and all of Stafford Cliff's *The Way We Live* books," says Kaitlyn.

2 Build confidence. "Go on eBay and buy design books from the 1990s or earlier, when nothing looked the same and everyone had their own unique style," Kaitlyn advises.

3 Shop accordingly. "Don't think too much about if something will 'go,'" Kaitlyn advises. "When you buy things that you like, all the items make sense because that is your taste."

Right: Kaitlyn narrowly missed out on scoring twin Le Corbusier chairs at a thrift shop, but managed to snag at least one of them for her living room. Antique American and English desks are a foil to the more modern sideboard and coffee table, all of which display books as well as favorite finds from over the years. "Note the Barbra Streisand book," Kaitlyn hints. "There are lots of hidden 'Barbra' items around the house. She's my idol!"

Left and below: "I love mixing these insanely ornate and priceless pieces next to naïve art," says Kaitlyn of the "so old, so magical" thrifted tall dresser flanked by antique chairs of varying provenance. Two antique quilts found at an estate sale dictated using twin beds in "the most fun room in the house," as Kaitlyn describes the kids' room.

"You want your house to be welcoming, cozy, comfortable...and not too precious."

Above: Since their home was built in 1963, Kaitlyn wanted the modernized bathroom to feel like it was part of that period. "Women used to pride themselves on their brightly colored bathrooms with bold clashing colors and tiles." she notes. "So I did that too!"

Above: Hidden gems in the master bedroom include antique French painted side tables bearing gold fleur-de-lis motifs on top (a spindle stool holds books and electronics that are too big for the dainty surface), as well as a recent addition: an antique forest fire painting. "It has the heaviest patina, but I'll never refurbish it because it gives off this spooky burnt vibe," says Kaitlyn.

noting that when there's a will, there's a way. And then there's the mid-century dining set and buffet from Nate's grandmother, who has joined them for meals around that very table and talked about its provenance. "So cool," Kaitlyn observes.

Moreover, "I love the fact that our house is unique to my family, our needs, our creativity and our style," says Kaitlyn. "I also love that my kids are growing up in a visually stimulating environment, whether they realize it or not," she laughs. But she adds that it extends beyond that: "You want your home to be welcoming, cozy, comfortable...and not too precious," she says. A friend and realtor/estate agent has picked up on that engaging vibe, describing the home as "a great place to be on a rainy day." To Kaitlyn, that was the highest compliment she could receive.

Opposite: Art and pottery—which Jana both collects and creates—are highlighted in this living-room vignette. "All my statuary wear necklaces," she says (these ones are made from Mexican clay and shell). A primitive vase holds coral-like branches that a neighbor found in her yard and painted.

Below right: A friend chased down, literally, one of Jana's favorite possessions: a genuine tumbleweed that sits in the fireplace. Above it, glass flowers from Mexico and vintage candlesticks mingle with her own artwork.

"For lack of a better word, my style is definitely eclectic," says Tyler native Jana Jamison of the home she shares with her husband, Bill, dog, Ruby, and Eartha Kitt, the cat. They moved into the park-side abode a decade ago, and since then Jana has come to appreciate how the neighborhood attracts lots of visitors, and is "varied in style of home and people," as she describes it, which is a bit of foreshadowing in how her own style has evolved. Back in the '90s, she turned to favorite magazines as she developed her taste, and these days the internet "has blown open new views and inspirations," she observes. But after years of living and learning and doing, these days she's equally inspired by her friends and surroundings. In other words, she's learned to trust herself.

Masterful in the Mix

There's something artful to behold in every corner of this east Texas home. "Nothing fine," declares owner Jana Jamison, who loves to search out the perfectly imperfect, and relishes using her finds to create—and recreate; more about that later—interior spaces that are equal parts interesting and inviting.

The living room reveals how Jana likes to mix it up. Tramp art, textiles, handicrafts and furnishings from antique to modern are combined to delight the eye. "I love the light in this room and it's a great place to visit with friends," she says.

Make It Personal

Steal this idea! Have a piece of glass cut to fit a tabletop so that you can show off favorite photos and ephemera underneath it.

" 'Things' are interesting and so much fun, but they can't be more important or precious than the people meant to enjoy them."

"I loved 'decorating' my room as a child," says Jana, whose urge to embellish has apparently always been with her. "As a young homeowner, though, I felt like there were specific boundaries," she says. "Our town was very 'English barley twist' and traditional, and I thought my house needed to look like a mature grown-up's home," she says, with a laugh. "The older I got, the more I was exposed to through friends and less mainstream sources, and I realized a home could be welcoming, interesting, quirky, personal...and still be put together." So these days, Jana says, she takes a more relaxed approach.

That attitude adjustment plays out in a home filled with interesting finds, largely bearing some kind of handcraftsmanship—Jana herself is a "maker" who works in mediums from needlework to paint to clay—but nothing so idolized as to provoke anxiety. "'Things' are interesting and so much fun, but they can't be more important or precious than the people meant to enjoy them," Jana declares. "If something breaks, it is thrown away or repaired, but not lamented," she adds. That said, she doesn't eschew sentimentality.

Creating Dynamic Displays

1 Grouping your collectibles is one of the easiest ways to create impact, whether achieved through hanging pictures on a gallery wall, lining up sculptural silhouettes on a shelf or gathering "littles" in a big glass bowl. Or try organizing by color and/or shape.

2 Be a show-off. Highlight a prized painting with a picture light, or tuck in battery-operated LED "candles" beside glazed and glass surfaces to make them shimmer. Place a cool curiosity under a tall cloche where it commands attention (and inspection).

3 Master the vignette. There may not be a foolproof formula, but this kind of display benefits from variety. Think: wood + metal + glass; tall, medium and short; shiny, matte and textured.

Opposite: Prized for its pattern variety, brown transferware is one of Jana's oldest collections. In a hallway, artfully displayed platters and butter pats surround a child-size hutch/dresser fashioned from old crates. It holds—what else?—children's transferware!

Above left: "In a Dream" is what Jana named the hooked rug she created based on actual dreams she's had. Lined up above it is a row of Renwal dollhouse dolls from the 1940s that belonged to a friend.

Above right: On the landing, another rug project is surrounded by tin-can chairs. "They were a craft in the 1960s and '70s, and no two are ever alike," says Jana, who usually finds them one at a time in thrift shops.

Take the dining table that her father made, for instance. After years of use, Jana refinished the top, covering it with an array of photos. "I call it 'Dinner with Family,'" she says. "I treasure that." Another keeper is a swivel chair she and her husband inherited from his grandmother. "All the kids spun around on it," Jana says. "I will never get rid of that."

But she may move it around. To keep rooms from becoming stale, Jana regularly rotates furniture from room to room, and confesses that she's willing to sell and replace things more often than others might be. It's a habit she acquired as an antidote to her love of thrifting. "I am not on the hunt for anything in particular, but I am always looking," she admits, noting that she's a "fall-in-love" kind of buyer. "Because I am a collector and enjoy so many things, I make myself let go of them. I enjoy them for a season, then I let someone else enjoy them. The only thing I am married to is my husband."

And she upholds that good-humored distinction between what she likes and what she loves when she's on the hunt. "I am absolutely not a purist; I do not care about imperfections," Jana says. "In fact, I find some things beautiful precisely because they are imperfect and someone still saved them."

Right: Brown and green tones factor in throughout Jana's home, and this combo's calming effects are welcome in the bedroom, where antique shutters and a pair of chairs flank a pine hutch/dresser filled with more Mexican pottery and jugs.

Have Fun

Terra-cotta flower pots in the bedroom? Yes! Athens Tile and Pottery stopped making these ones in 1968, so Jana elevated them to sculpture status.

Among the things that have caught her eye enough to collect include brown transferware, tramp art, hat forms, art pottery and even tin-can chairs. But "My biggest decorating love is art and handmade items," Jana reveals. "I have collected old oil paintings for years, but also incorporate mid-century art, primitive paintings and contemporary work. Pottery is another handmade medium that makes my heart skip," she adds. "I have art made by friends and things I have made too. Nothing fine or expensive, but precious in a joyous sense to me." Accordingly, this shows up in every single room of her house, where she has become a veritable mix master. "Old with new, 'high' with 'low,' shiny with matte, primitive with modern; mixing is what keeps everything interesting," Jana says. "I want people to feel welcome when they walk in the door, and I want that feeling to permeate my home."

With its antique oil paintings, quirky finds like a dress-form floor lamp and a tabletop light with an old wallpaper roller forming the base, and a wicker desk topped with an antique rug, Jana says their bedroom is a great place to dream—awake or asleep!

More than a century after being built, a cobbled-together farmhouse has undergone an artful reinterpretation that takes advantage of its verdant surroundings just steps from the idyllic historic downtown square in McKinney, Texas.

Farm Fresh

Opposite: With rugged brick floors and light pouring in from both sides, the breezeway that connects the garage to the house makes a great painting studio for Angie, who also likes to keep plants there.

Above: Vibrant Italian tomato cans hold brushes atop a tool chest that stashes more supplies. Angie found the vintage painter's palette at Round Top.

Former antiques dealer and occasional interior designer Angie Cavalier and her husband, Michael, appreciate a house with a story to tell, and theirs has two. The original home was a simple farmhouse built in the 1890s, but about a decade later, the man who built it moved another small farmhouse from a neighboring community onto the property and combined it with the original structure. The longtime McKinney residents had always loved the home's location, just a couple of tree-lined blocks from the buzzy downtown square and yet private and small-town feeling thanks to its decent-size lot and surrounding mature shade trees. So when it became available a decade ago, the pair felt the pull to purchase it, but it would be a while before they could call it home...or at least the home they envisioned.

While ideally situated, they found that the house had a hodgepodge of narrow hallways with too many doors and a layout that did not make sense. "We spent two years taking down walls and adding support where needed,

Break the Rules

Can you have dogs and kids and white furniture at the same time? Angie does, because she opts for slipcovered pieces, so all she needs is a washing machine when life happens.

Left and above: A "flying bird's nest," as Angie describes the living room's light fixture, is perched over a seating area designed for conversation. The floating fireplace was a surprise find—it had been hidden inside a wall.

Spot Potential

Ordinary items can become showstoppers when displayed en masse, like these stone pendants that define the dining area. Hint, if you haven't heard: odd numbers work best for good groupings.

Opposite: Angie had a welder craft a frame for a large antique factory window that she found. It's been fashioned into an interesting room divider that doesn't interrupt the home's generous natural light and open flow.

adding and subtracting windows and completely reworking the flow of the house," says Angie. They were even willing to sacrifice storage to capitalize on spacious, light-flooded rooms. "I really wanted to have a very open kitchen with lots of windows, so I decided to go without upper cabinets," Angie cites as an example. "I have had to get very creative with kitchen storage using vintage wire baskets and metal boxes and creating a very hardworking pantry. My motto has been 'everything you need and not much that you don't.'"

Left: In the kitchen, Angie was happy to forfeit storage in exchange for sweeping backyard and garden views. The island is actually a farm table that was found outside of a barn in England.

Above: An antique baker's table got a new lease on life when Angie had its legs extended to counter height and marble cut for the top. Above it, the first quote she put on the giant chalkboard she had installed still remains seven years later.

Above: An antique bottle-drying rack makes use of vertical space to store aprons and keep coffee mugs always ready to grab.

The design ethic paid off; for Angie, the next best thing to being in her beloved backyard is enjoying its view from the kitchen.

Indeed, the home speaks to simple joys. This "reformed collector," as Angie describes herself, used to scoop up "antique everything—mercury glass, transferware, ironstone, silver, tole trays, majolica, shell art...the list went on and on," she says. At 41, though, she was diagnosed with breast cancer. "After a three-year upheaval of my life, I realized that I no longer wanted all of that 'stuff,'" she says. These days, she can appreciate something without having to bring it home. Unless it's a book. "I am a collector with a tendency toward hoarding," she admits, "and I also have a weakness for vintage oil paintings and antique religious items. But I have learned to be much more discerning about what comes home with me," she concludes.

Part of that perspective also comes from having expanded her shopping opportunities. "When I was younger, and before I had traveled very much,

Why It Pays
To Travel

1 Visiting the other side of the country or a far-off part of the world opens your eyes to new possibilities. Angie found that a trip to Paris taught her how to mix antiques with contemporary items. "They do that so well in Europe," she notes. "They embrace the modern while still preserving and celebrating their history."

2 For collectors, visiting a region where something was famously made—think Amish quilts or mid-century modern furniture—can offer the luxury of varied and quality choices.

3 Don't underestimate prize finds with an exotic backstory. There's something fun about being able to say, "Oh that? I found it in…"

"I like to imagine the people who loved something before I did. It sort of makes me feel like a caretaker of the past."

I was influenced by design books and magazines for the most part," Angie confesses. Now a seasoned traveler, she is influenced by the places she has been and the people she's met along the way. "My first trip to Paris imbued me with a newfound love of mixing antiques with contemporary items," she says. "They do that so well in Europe." In truth, her love affair with antiques and design started long before she ever crossed the Atlantic. "My mom would drag my sister and me to antiques malls. She was always looking for a bargain and I think she rearranged the furniture once a month!" Angie laughs. But it fueled her love of searching for a diamond in the rough, and discovering its backstory. "I like to imagine the people who loved something before I did,"

Above and opposite: Although she considers herself a reformed collector, Angie admits that she still has a big problem saying no to books. "I originally bought this antique French ladder to help reach the books on higher shelves," she reports, "but it has become an extension of the bookcase now!"

"Kind of like wearing diamonds with blue jeans and a white T-shirt," as Angie describes it, she paired an ornate chandelier with modern linens and clean lines to keep the master bedroom spare and serene.

dream

"I think the objects that we enjoy surrounding ourselves with are a reflection of our constantly changing and evolving lives."

Above left: Angie found the chandelier that now crowns the clawfoot tub in their master bathroom at one of Paris's famous brocantes. She loved it enough to haul it all the way home in her carry-on bag.

Above right: A patchwork of colorful encaustic tiles and a floating quartz sink turn this powder room—"a perfect place to do something different," notes Angie—into a hidden gem.

Angie says. "It makes me feel like a caretaker of the past. And there is no better way to take care of our environment than to use antiques to furnish your home. Most of my favorite pieces have been around for over 100 years and are just getting started."

And that's a good thing, because it leaves room for growth. These days, Angie describes her taste as eclectic, with a soft spot for the perfectly imperfect. "I think the objects that we enjoy surrounding ourselves with are a reflection of our constantly changing and evolving lives," she says. "Home should be where you come to relax and unwind. My greatest compliment is when someone tells me that they feel completely at ease in our home."

JACQUES COUSTEAU
THE OCEAN WORLD

When he bought a weekend retreat in a sleepy Delaware beachside town in 2016, this New York mover and shaker couldn't have guessed how soon a devastating world event would end up changing his life...for the better.

Full Steam Ahead

Opposite: In the cozy den, sink-into English armchairs rest below the horizon of vintage ship and boat paintings that are part of Memo's first and largest collection.

Above right: Completed in the late 1700s but picked up many years later in Canada, the painting over the cabinet that houses vintage ironstone and blue-and-white white ceramics is the oldest in the home.

Sometimes having a side hustle can pay off in more ways than one. Just ask Memo Faraj, who was holding down a full-time career in New York City's fashion industry but dabbling in art and design passion projects. When the pandemic hit and everything shut down, it opened up an opportunity to make those passions his main focus as he retreated to the coastal getaway. It has since become his full-time residence where he divides his time between interior design and decorating work and pursuing his love of painting.

Originally charmed by the home's character and over 200-year-old history—it was built from recycled wood from ships, was at one point a church rectory and is on the National Register of Historic Places—Memo says that there was no adjustment period settling in: "This house was magic from the moment I set foot inside. It immediately felt like it belonged to me."

Left: *"The living room is the center of the home and where I entertain," says Memo, who hauled the vintage Persian wool rug from New York one weekend. The antique dresser in the corner houses art supplies and has his collection of quartz obelisks on top.*

Collecting on a Budget

1 Develop a system. Memo ranks his finds out of 10. "If it's an 8, 9 or 10 on the scale of how much I want or love it, I usually buy it," he says. "Anything below an 8, I move on."

2 Don't settle for second best. Be patient and save up, he advises. "You always end up going back and buying the item you wanted in the first place anyway, so save yourself the time and money."

3 Be consistent, shop often and look everywhere. "I find amazing things in all sorts of places; ceramic treasures mixed into the gardening section or wooden sculptures in the kids' section," Memo says.

Left: A vintage painter's bench serves as the living room's coffee table, where an antique wooden trunk offers a place to stash candles and more. The antique seascape in a gilded frame was a $50 thrift-shop score.

Below: With its headstone-like shape, an antique hand-painted wooden sign is a real eye-catcher on the dining room wall. An old pair of wooden phoenixes presides over the doorway into the living room.

Opposite: Formerly used for display in a Ralph Lauren shop, Memo picked up the oversize vintage lawyer's table at a sample sale. He paired it with a mix of vintage captain's and modern farm chairs, and refashioned a modern poker table light to illuminate both the table and the ceiling.

"Quality doesn't have to mean expensive. Do your research and invest in pieces that will stand the test of time."

But that doesn't mean he hasn't put his stamp on it. While Memo had a light hand in renovations so as not to further misguided modernizations done by previous owners, he's made his mark with some cosmetic upgrades and accessorized heavily with his favorite thing: art.

A talented painter who uses acrylics, oils, pastels and charcoal to tap into his favorite subjects of science and nature—"Coral and entomology are huge inspirations for me," he says—Memo loves the power of art to transport you to different times and places. Paintings are his favorite thing to collect. "I started with nautical and it has expanded into many genres, though I am always looking for ship paintings. I love them and, as they are my largest collection, I have over 100 pieces," he confesses, adding that he's now quite choosy when it comes to making any additions. A self-described maximalist, he also loves collecting handmade ceramics, sculptures, bowls and studio pottery. "Every room, every corner in my home has some form of art," says Memo. "I can't imagine it any other way."

Luckily, he can imagine practicing restraint when shopping, which he does "anywhere and everywhere," from flea markets, estate sales and auctions to online haunts like Facebook Marketplace, eBay and Etsy. "I abide by the 'one-in, one-out' rule," he says. "It's important I maintain balance so that the collection doesn't overwhelm." And it's important to balance the budget too, a challenge that he's met by learning to spot quality items at affordable

Break the Rules

Memo says: "If you love the frame and hate the art, buy it. I collect so much of both and interchange them!"

"The originality of antiques brings something special into a space that you can't achieve with new things."

Opposite: Eclectic travels are what inspired the guest-room décor, where a wooden ceremonial headdress cozies up to a vintage green dresser topped with a modern cement lamp and delicate Staffordshire birds.

Above: Natural textures like organic cotton bedding, vintage linen shams/decorative pillowcases and a cashmere throw bring modern luxury to the antique spindle bed that grounds the guest room.

secondhand sources, and by learning to pace himself. "I pick and choose what I want to prioritize," he says. "I have a million ideas and I will have many years to work my way through each of them."

In the meantime, Memo continues to layer favorite finds that are not destined for the wall into tabletop vignettes and bookcases, displaying smaller artworks on vintage easels and ceramics under a cloche or on top of a stack of books, all with an eye to accessibility. "It allows my friends to pick something up and explore it," he says, noting that art and artifacts should be interactive and fun. "It's not a museum!" Memo jokes of his collection-filled home. "I want someone to visit and instantly feel welcome and at ease, to explore and be excited, to make memories and to want to come back," he says. "Isn't that the true test of a home?"

After years in New York City's fashion industry, a dyed-in-the-wool vintage lover decided to try a country look by heading upstate, where she found an old home that had once been a hotel and post office. It would take some tailoring, but it had all the makings of a good fit.

American Idyll

Opposite: A hand-hewn barn beam from the 1850s anchors this corner of the living room. The naïve landscape oil painting tells the story of all the elements surrounding it.

Above right: Melanie envisioned this old campaign desk as something that would have been in the hotel in the 1880s. The charming corgi pastels above it were Salvation Army store finds.

It's not uncommon for thrifting types to get the bug at an early age, as was the case for Melanie Bendavid, who was bitten—and smitten—after hitting a New Jersey flea market as a 12-year-old. What may be less common, though, is how it stuck with her, even shaping her professional life. On that first shopping venture, she picked up an old portrait of a girl (which she still has); then, as a high-schooler, she'd zero in on cool clothing to tailor into her own duds. But she really took it to the next level when she channeled her passions into a career at Ralph Lauren, researching vintage clothing and shopping for antiques that would help to shape the look of the iconic brand. When she was ready for her next act, away from New York City life, she decided to check out the Catskill region, where, an hour after it was listed, she "checked into" the home she has since worked with her partner, Michael Randels, to restore.

Left: Salvaged cupboards and a mantel that originally came from Bobby Kennedy's home were incorporated to recreate the look of a traditional cooking fireplace (and warming spot for Betty, the rescue dog).

Opposite: The stairway was opened up to create an airy space; photos of the original builders grace its walls. Nature is brought indoors by way of landscape portraits, carved deer heads, brass insects and painted birds.

Spot Potential

Doors on cabinets and cupboards let you play hide-and-seek. Here, a new TV over the fireplace is concealed by a set of old paneled doors.

"The old house was stripped of any original elements, so I had to reimagine what it might have looked like in 1868 when it was constructed," recalls Melanie. Luckily, she uncovered some helpful clues while renovating. "When I bought it, I didn't realize the house had dropped ceilings with tiles," she says. "We were pleasantly surprised to find what was revealed underneath during demo: 11-ft/3.35m ceilings and hidden transom and sidelight windows at the entrance." Amazingly, the original glass from 1868 was found intact. This prompted further investigation and extensive research into the

Left: Using reclaimed barnwood, Michael lovingly crafted a 9-ft/2.7m farm table that can seat 10. The painted country dining chairs around it were won at an auction in rural Vermont.

Above: The honeybee study was hand-painted by a local artist. Found in his attic at a yard sale, it was originally painted as a ceiling panel for a New York speakeasy.

Have Fun

Set a little scene. Antique rug beaters lining the hallway wall pay tribute to the sisters who maintained the hotel in the 1800s.

Opposite: In what might be the most incredible score of all time, Melanie found the entire kitchen—right down to the six-burner stove—at a local salvage business. Above the cabinets are her ever-growing collection of antique saltware crocks and white enamel kitchenware.

history of the old hotel. "Michael did his best to focus on the integrity of the structure and bring it back to its original splendor and craftsmanship," says Melanie, who notes that he conceived and constructed the "dream design" by mirroring the original post-and-beam construction of the interior.

Melanie responded in kind by filling each room with character-rich antiques found at largely local sources—"My treasures come from every kind of sale.

I brake for everything!" she says—that sync with the age of the house. Indeed, finds from the famous Brimfield Antique Flea Market mingle with incredible salvage scores to lend notes of authenticity throughout. And even more locally sourced are the birds' nests, feathers, moth wings and greenery that Melanie finds around the property and brings inside to display here and there. "I love to forage and to bring the seasonal organic elements indoors," she says. "It is very soothing for me to surround myself with elements of nature after spending so many years in the city." And she has imbued her rooms with that calming sense by using a color palette grounded in earthy neutrals and enhanced by hues fabricated by what you might call local artists: all of the interior wall, door and ceiling colors were inspired by fresh chicken eggs from a friend's farm.

All of Melanie and Michael's efforts have combined to create a cozy home that pays tribute to the past while being practical and livable today. And their diligence was rewarded with some help along the way, as they developed a

Success With Salvage

1 Hunt in offbeat spots. It's not a rule, but in general, the nicer the shop, the higher the prices. If you're looking for a single, specific item in great condition, this may be the way to go. But if you get into junkyards, old barns and basements, you may score some great deals if you're willing to put in a little elbow grease.

2 Get help. Sought-after items like vintage lighting or bathroom fixtures can bring authentic old character to rooms, but involve a pro to ensure wiring and plumbing are new and safe for use today.

3 Make alterations. When Melanie found a small wooden table in a back field at Brimfield, she envisioned a coffee table, so had its legs cut down accordingly.

Above: On the bedroom closet door hangs a 1940s charmeuse and lace slip that belonged to Melanie's mother. "I love to mix opulent with rustic. I think the two elements complement and ground one another," she observes.

Below: A collection of African trading beads from Brimfield hangs next to antique skeleton keys, a nod to the long-gone days when the house was a hotel.

Opposite: A walk-through cedar closet built by Michael holds personal mementos, friends' artwork, portraits and old paintings. "I believe that closets and bathrooms are most important to decorate," Melanie says.

A child-size chair wears a flour sack that Melanie found in an old barn. A good soaking revealed the most beautiful stenciling on the fabric, she says. And although she wouldn't describe herself as "a lacy person," the delicate curtain panels were perfect for filtering light into the bedroom.

Above left: *A weathered bench that offers a perfect perch for potted plants makes the bathroom feel like a greenhouse, Melanie says. She recovered the small bench below with woven upholstery webbing.*

Above right: *Artwork in the bathroom includes antique shell coin purses, which were popular Victorian souvenirs in seaside towns. Apothecary and other bottles were discovered (and cleaned up) during a remodeling excavation.*

"My treasures come from every kind of sale. I brake for everything!"

great relationship with direct ancestors of the original builders and family that lived in and ran the hotel (who reunited at the property a few years ago). But Melanie doesn't take that as a sign that their work is complete. Like any good caretaker of an historic home, she's happy to play her part in its evolution. "It will never really be done," she says.

Sources

Here's a guide to some of the people, places and items in this book. A note, with vintage and antique items there is no guarantee of availability; consider this a starting point for your hunt.

HOMEOWNERS

Rozana and Patrick Gillogly
throughtheportholeshop.com
@throughtheporthole

Deborah Harold
deborahharold.com

Kirsten Tangeros
@kooselie

Melissa Parks
Warehouse 55
Aurora, IL
warehouse55.shop
@megillicutti

Molly Bechert Kipp
@the.polo.house

Johanna Brannan Lowe
@johannalowe
@parchmenthouse
@parchmentstudio

Kaitlyn Coffee
kaitlyn.coffee
@harrisvintage

Jana Jamison
@jrjami

Angie Cavalier
@mymckinneyfarmhouse

Melanie Bendavid
@mel_b_111

Memo Faraj
memofaraj.com
@lecabinetofcuriosity

FLEA MARKETS & ANTIQUES SHOWS

Barnhouse Chicks Market Pop-Ups
Southern CA
@barnhousechicksmarket

Brimfield Antique Flea Markets
Brimfield, MA
brimfieldantiquefleamarket.com

Elkhorn Antique Flea Market
Elkhorn, WI
elkhornantiquefleamarket.com

First Monday Canton
Canton, TX
firstmondaycanton.com

Junk Bonanza
Shakopee, MN
junkbonanza.com

Long Beach Antique Market
Long Beach, CA
longbeachantiquemarket.com

Randolph Street Market
Chicago, IL
randolphstreetmarket.com

Rose Bowl Flea Market
Pasadena, CA
rgcshows.com

Round Top and Warrenton Antique Shows
Round Top and Warrenton, TX
antiqueweekend.com

Santa Monica Airport Antique Market
Santa Monica, CA
santamonicaairportantiquemarket.com

Springfield Antique Show + Flea Market
Springfield, OH
jenkinsandco.com/springfield-antique-show

SHOPS

Some brick-and-mortar shops offer multiple locations plus online shopping

Amber Interiors Design Studio
Calabasas, CA
amberinteriordesign.com

Architectural Anarchy
Chicago, IL
@architecturalanarchy

Big Daddy's Antiques
Los Angeles, CA
@bigdaddysantiques

Blue Moon Vintage Market
Westville, IN
bluemoonvintagemarket.com

Blue Springs Home
Costa Mesa, CA
bluespringshome.com

Broadway Antique Market
Chicago, IL
@bamchicago

Brown Elephant Resale Shops
Chicago, IL
@brownelephant

Camps & Cottages
Laguna Beach, CA
camps-cottages.com

Curiosities
Dallas, TX
getcuriosities.com

Dial M for Modern
Chicago, IL
dialmformodern.com

Ethel's Treasure Quest
Tyler, TX
FB EthelsTreasureQuest

The Find Consignments
Costa Mesa, CA
@thefindconsignments

Housing Works Thrift Shops
Brooklyn and New York City, NY
housingworks.org

Jayson Home (Vintage Collections)
Chicago, IL
jaysonhome.com

Juxtaposition Home
Newport Beach, CA
juxtaposition.com

Heritage Trail Mercantile
Northfield, IL
heritagetrailmall.com

Layered by Paige Elise
Costa Mesa, CA
layeredbypaigeelise.com

Lee Hartwell Antiques
Callicoon, New York
@leehartwellantiques

LuLa B's Antique Mall
Dallas, TX
@lulabsdd

Magnolia Mews Consignment
Newport Beach, CA
magnoliamews.com

The Mart Collective
Venice, CA
themartcollective.com

Meg Made
Chicago, IL
megmade.com

Modified Home
Dallas, TX
@modified_home

Olde Good Things
New York City, NY and Los Angeles, CA and Scranton, PA
ogtstore.com

Restore-Habitat for Humanity
Chicago, IL
habitatchicago.org/restore

Robandt Antiques
Buchanan, MI
alanrobandt.com

Salvage One
Chicago, IL
salvageone.com

Scout Design
Andersonville, IL
@scoutdesign

Sofa U Love
Locations throughout CA
sofaulove.com

Sojourn
Sawyer, MI
@sojourn.sawyer

South Loop Loft
Chicago, IL
thesouthlooploft.com

Sweet William Antique Mall
Colorado Springs, CO
sweetwilliamantiquemall.com

Tribute
Chicago IL
@tribute.chicago

Trilogy Antiques + Design
Three Oaks, MI
@trilogyantiques

Urban Americana
Long Beach, CA
urbanamericana.com

Warehouse 55
Aurora and Chicago, IL
warehouse55.shop

The Well Summerland
Summerland, CA
@thewellsummerland

The Willows
Phoenix, AZ
willowsdesign.com

ONLINE ONLY

1st DIBS
1stdibs.com

Alice Lane Home Collection
alicelanehome.com

Beata Heuman
shoppa.beataheuman.com

Chairish
chairish.com

Distinctive Chesterfields
distinctivechesterfields.com

Ebay
ebay.com

Etsy
etsy.com

Everything but the House
ebth.com

Live Auctioneers
liveauctioneers.com

Rouse Home
rousehome.com

Vintiques midcentury
@Vintiquesmidcentury

Facebook Marketplace
facebook.com/marketplace

ART

Aliya Sadaf
@aliyah.sadaf

Amanda Carol
@amandacarolofficial

Denise Dietz
@denisedietzart

Drew Ernst
drewernstart.com

Jena Traversa
@jena_traversa

Kader Boly
@kaderboly

Lucy Slivinski
lucyslivinski.com

Memor
shopmemor.com

Sarah Whalen
@sarahwhalen.studio

RUGS

Beni Rugs
benirugs.com

Cappelen Dimyr
cappelendimyr.com

Moroccan Treso Designs
etsy.com/shop/MoroccanTresoDesigns

Old New House
oldnewhouse.com

DESIGN/BUILD

Build TX Solutions (Kitchen Remodel—Coffee)
buildtx-solutions.com

Concrete Collaborative
(Concrete and Terrazzo Finishes)
concrete-collaborative.com

Crystal Blackshaw Interiors
(Collaborating Designer—Bechert Kipp)
crystalblackshaw.com

Delightful Designs
(Window Treatments)
Dallas, TX
delightfuldesigns.net

Garza Interiors
(Collaborating Designer—Coffee)
garzainteriors.co

Hygge and West
(Wallpaper and Home Goods)
hyggeandwest.com

Mulberry Home
(Fabrics and Wall Coverings)
@mulberry_home

Index

Page numbers in *italic* refer to the illustrations

Picture Credits

All photography by Edmund Barr (@edmundbarrphotography, edmundbarr.com) unless otherwise stated.

1, **2** and **3 centre** The home of Memo Faraj, styled by Frances Bailey @Francesfinds and francesbailey.com, photographed by John Bessler @johneeebee, johnbesslerphoto.com; **3 left** The home of Johanna Brannan Lowe, styled by Johanna Lowe @johannalowe, johannalowe.com; **3 right** The home of Deborah Harold; **4** The home of Kaitlyn and Nate Coffee, styled by Kaitlyn Coffee @kaityncoffeecreative, kaitlyn.coffee; **5** The home of Johanna Brannan Lowe, styled by Johanna Lowe @johannalowe, johannalowe.com; **6** and **7 right** The home of Memo Faraj, styled by Frances Bailey @Francesfinds and francesbailey.com, photographed by John Bessler @johneeebee, johnbesslerphoto.com; **7 left** The home of Angie and Michael Cavalier; **8** The home of Kaitlyn and Nate Coffee, styled by Kaitlyn Coffee @kaityncoffeecreative, kaitlyn.coffee; **10** The home of Johanna Brannan Lowe, styled by Johanna Lowe @johannalowe, johannalowe.com; **11 above right** The home of Kirsten Tangeros and Chris Thomas, styled by Melissa Parks @megillicutti; **11 below left** The home of Melanie Bendavid and Michael Randels, styled by Raina Kattelson @rainakattelson, rainakattelson.com and photographed by John Bessler @johneeebee, johnbesslerphoto.com; **12 above** The home of Memo Faraj, styled by Frances Bailey @Francesfinds and francesbailey.com, photographed by John Bessler @johneeebee, johnbesslerphoto.com; **12 below** The home of Rozana and Patrick Gillogly; **13** The home of Kirsten Tangeros and Chris Thomas, styled by Melissa Parks @megillicutti; **14** The home of Brian Hickman; **15 above left** The home of Jana and Bill Jamison; **15 below centre** and **right** The home of Memo Faraj, styled by Frances Bailey @Francesfinds and francesbailey.com, photographed by John Bessler @johneeebee, johnbesslerphoto.com; **16 right** The home of Jana and Bill Jamison; **16 left** and **17 above left** The home of Rozana and Patrick Gillogly; **17 below left** The home of Melissa and Jerry Parks, styled by Melissa Parks @megillicutti; **17 right** The home of Jana and Bill Jamison; **18 above left** and **below centre** The home of Memo Faraj, styled by Frances Bailey @Francesfinds and francesbailey.com, photographed by John Bessler @johneeebee, johnbesslerphoto.com; **18 below left** The home of Rozana and Patrick Gillogly; **19** and **20** The home of Memo Faraj, styled by Frances Bailey @Francesfinds and francesbailey.com, photographed by John Bessler @johneeebee, johnbesslerphoto.com; **22–35** The home of Brian Hickman; **36–45** The home of Rozana and Patrick Gillogly; **46–55** The home of Deborah Harold; **56–67** The home of Kirsten Tangeros and Chris Thomas, styled by Melissa Parks @megillicutti; **68–79** The home of Melissa and Jerry Parks, styled by Melissa Parks @megillicutti; **80–93** The home of Molly and Nate Kipp, styled by Melissa Parks @megillicutti; **94–103** The home of Johanna Brannan Lowe, styled by Johanna Lowe @johannalowe, johannalowe.com; **104–113** The home of Kaitlyn and Nate Coffee, styled by Kaitlyn Coffee @kaityncoffeecreative, kaitlyn.coffee; **114–123** The home of Jana and Bill Jamison; **124–137** The home of Angie and Michael Cavalier; **138–145** The home of Memo Faraj, styled by Frances Bailey @ Francesfinds and francesbailey.com, photographed by John Bessler @johneeebee, johnbesslerphoto.com; **146–157** The home of Melanie Bendavid and Michael Randels, styled by Raina Kattelson @rainakattelson, rainakattelson.com and photographed by John Bessler @johneeebee, johnbesslerphoto.com.

Acknowledgments

This book might still be a figment of my imagination if it wasn't for my dear friend and author Fifi O'Neill, who gave me the courage to step out of my comfort zone and guided me along the way. Thank you to the crew at Ryland Peters & Small; Annabel Morgan for giving a newbie a shot and enthusiastically leading a dream team of Paul Tilby, Sally Powell, Leslie Harrington and Gordana Simakovic. I am proud of what we created together.

Photographer extraordinaire Edmund Barr maintained a can-do attitude when I asked for the impossible. And thanks to John Bessler for his beautiful images of our East Coast homes. You both brought this project to colorful life. I am grateful to my talented friends Janet Mowat and Jodi Zucker for their editorial guidance that helped me find my voice. Thanks, too, to Melissa Parks for finding home candidates to get just the right mix. And to Leslie of Leslie Stoker Literary, thanks for translating all the contractual fine print.

A sincere thank you goes to the homeowners who generously allowed us to capture their homes just as they were and share personal stories and unique insights with us. They are the soul of this book. I also offer a heartfelt thank you to all the super-talented contributors, staff, vendors, peers and followers who joined me in my journey to promote the gospel of vintage over the years.

I am blessed to have a loving support system of family and friends. While I can't say that my kids, Taylor and Tyson, understood my attraction to salvaging and reinventing the old and worn when they were younger, today they are my rock-star cheerleaders. The journey is sweeter and more satisfying knowing they are by my side.

I hope you will join me for community, creativity and inspiration at lived-instyle.com and on social media @livedinstylemag.

Cheers to *Lived-In Style* and all things vintage!